Samsung Galaxy A16 5G Simplified User Guide For Beginners and Seniors

A Detailed Manual With Tips, Tricks and Directional Screenshots For Setup and Configuration

Peterson Clever

Table of Contents

13

Introduction

The Samsung Galaxy A16 – A New Era of Innovation at Your Fingertips

In the ever-evolving world of smartphones, where technology moves at lightning speed and expectations constantly rise, Samsung has once again redefined what it means to stay connected, entertained, and productive. Enter the Samsung Galaxy A16, a device that not only meets the needs of today's smartphone user but anticipates the demands of tomorrow.

This book takes you on a journey through the world of the Galaxy A16—a stunning blend of sleek design, powerful performance, and cutting-edge technology. Whether you're a casual user looking for seamless daily experiences or a tech enthusiast craving innovation, the A16 has something for everyone. From its ultra-responsive display to its impressive camera system, this phone is built to enhance every aspect of your life.

As we dive into the details of the A16, we will explore its design philosophy, features, and capabilities that make it stand out in a crowded market. You'll discover how Samsung's commitment to quality and user-centric innovation shines through, ensuring that each feature—from its battery life to its processing power—delivers exactly what you need in a modern smartphone.

This is not just a phone; it's a window into the future of mobile technology. So, whether you're holding the device for the first time or looking to get the most out of your Galaxy A16, join us as we uncover what makes this device a true game-changer.

Chapter one
Configure your Phone

Your device makes use of an accessory called the Nano-SIM card. You might be able to use a SIM card you already have or use one you already have.

Install SIM/microSD card
Place the SIM card and optional microSD™ card (sold separately) into the tray with the gold contacts facing down.

Charge your device
Before turning on your device, charge it fully.

NOTE: The warranty does not cover damages caused by user usage, therefore please only use cables, batteries, chargers, and other accessories that have been approved by Samsung with your device. Using unapproved accessories might damage your device.

Charge the device battery

A robust rechargeable battery will comprise the Galaxy A16.

NOTE: If the charger stops working while charging, it's because it overheated. Don't worry, the phone's lifetime will be unaffected; simply remove the charger from the device and let it cool down.

Turn on your device

To activate the gadget, press the Side key. You shouldn't use a device that has a broken or cracked body until it's mended.

- o To activate the gadget, press and hold the side key for a few seconds.

- • To power off the device, press and hold the Side key. Then, tap the 🔘 Power off symbol on the screen.

- • Restart the device by tapping the 🔄 Restart symbol on the screen after pressing and holding the Side key.

Use the Setup Wizard

When you power up your smartphone for the first time, the Setup Wizard will guide you through the setup process.

To modify the default language, create an account, connect to a Wi-Fi network, and more, follow the on-screen instructions

Import data from an old device

With the Smart Switch, you can easily move media files, contacts, calendar events, photographs, videos, messages, notes, and music from one device to another. If Smart Switch isn't already installed on your device, you may easily download it. Smart Switch supports data transfer via USB, Wi-Fi, or PC.

1. To import data from an older device, open the Settings app, go to the Accounts and backup menu, and then hit the corresponding button.

2. Following the preceding step, adhere to the instructions displayed on the screen.

Lock or Unlock

When the screen expires, the lock screen locks automatically. To lock and unlock the device manually, press the Side key.

Side key/Fingerprint scanner
Press to lock.
Press to turn on the screen, and then swipe the screen to unlock it.

Accounts

Make an account and take care of it.

Add a Google account

Without logging into your Google account, you might not be able to access your Google Cloud Storage.

"Google Device Protection" is activated the moment you log into your Google account and configure a lock screen.

1. Go to 🔘 Accounts and backup > Manage accounts after opening the device's settings app.

2. Choose Google from the ╬ Add account drop-down box to link your Google account.

Add a Samsung account

After you log in with your Samsung account on the smartphone, you'll have full access to Samsung exclusive content.

o Go to your device's settings and find the Samsung account option.

Add an outlook account

After logging in, you'll have access to manage your inbox.

1. Find the 🔄 Accounts and backup option in the device's settings app, and then press Manage accounts.

2. Select Outlook from the ➕ Add account menu to add an Outlook account.

Set up voicemail

You have to configure the voicemail feature the first time you use it. The Phone app provides access to voicemail.

1. From the Apps screen, launch 📞 Phone by touching 📧 Voicemail or by pressing and holding the 1 button.

2. To set up a password, record your name, or say hello, just follow the on-screen prompts.

Navigation

You can use your fingertips or other non-metallic things to navigate the screen without using any force. The device's warranty does not cover damage caused by using a metallic item or applying excessive pressure to the screen.

Tap

To activate an item, lightly tap on it.

- Choose an item by clicking on it.
- Press and hold a picture for two seconds to enlarge or reduce its size.

Swipe

- Swipe horizontally or vertically across the screen to activate the swipe function.

- A vertical swipe from the lock screen's base will unlock the smartphone.

Drag and drop

- You can move items about by tapping and holding them, then dragging them to a different spot.

- Drag an app shortcut to the home screen to make it a shortcut there.

Zoom in and out

- To magnify the image, separate your fingers.
- To zoom out, join your fingers.

Press and hold

Simply pressing and holding an item will activate it.

- Press and hold a blank spot on your home screen to access the settings you choose.

Navigation bar

To move about on the smartphone, you may either utilize the navigation keys or the full screen gesture.

Recent apps   Back

Home

Navigation buttons

Just tap the button on the bottom of the screen to effortlessly browse the gadget.

1. Start up the settings app, and then go to the Display, navigation bar, and buttons menu.

2. Pressing Button order allows you to customize the placement of the Back, Home, and Recent buttons on the screen.

Navigation gestures

To make swiping on the screen your primary means of navigating, disable the buttons and enable navigation gestures.

1. Click on Display in the Settings menu, then touch on the Navigation bar. Finally, hit on Swipe gestures to enable the function.

2. Choose a setting to personalize:

- Additional choices: To choose a gesture type and sensitivity, tap the "More Options" icon.

- Hints for gestures: This function allows you to draw lines at the bottom of the screen to indicate the location of each gesture.

- An icon will appear in the bottom right corner of your screen when your smartphone is in Portrait mode; press this symbol to conceal the keyboard.

Customize your home screen

Improving the Home screen experience is as simple as adding widgets and applications that you use often.

App icons

The icons of your apps may be accessed from the Home screen by just clicking on them.

o When you're in the app, tap and hold the icon until you get the ⊕ Add to Home screen.

To remove the icon for an application:

o Pressing and holding the Home screen app you wish to uninstall will bring up the 🗑 Delete button.

NOTE: Erasing an app from the Home screen does not permanently delete it from your device.

Wallpaper

Set the background image to one of the system wallpapers or upload a photo of your own.

In order to insert a background picture, do the following:

1. Find ▦ Wallpapers & style on the Home screen by pressing and holding an empty area.

29

2. To see all of the wallpapers that are available, choose:

- To personalize the home screen and lock screen, click on their respective images.

- You may either use the pre-installed wallpapers or find and download new ones from Galaxy Themes in the "Wallpapers" section.

- Color palette: Select a palette that complements the wallpaper's color scheme.

- Turn on dark mode for your wallpaper by tapping the dark mode button and then following the on-screen prompts.

Themes

App icons, the home screen, wallpapers, and the lock screen may all be customized using downloadable themes.

1. To access the Home screen, press and hold a space.

2. Press to choose a theme. Before you download the theme, make sure you preview it.

3. Go to your library of downloaded themes by tapping on My Stuff and then selecting Themes.

4. Just pick a theme and hit the apply button.

Icons

The default system icons can be replaced with icons that you can download.

1. Tap and hold any location on the main screen.

2. Find a collection of icons you like, go to Themes > Icons, and then download them.

3. Browse your downloaded icons by going to >My things > Icons.

4. Hit the Apply button to put the chosen symbol into action.

Widgets

In order to add a widget on the home screen, please follow these steps:

1. While the Home screen is empty, press and hold a spot.

2. After tapping , click on a group of widgets to open them.

3. Select a widget from the list and then hit the Add button to add it to the Home screen.

Customize widgets

The widgets on the home screen may be customized to suit your needs.

- On the Home screen, press and hold the widget you wish to modify, and then choose an option from the list below:

- To make a stack, just place additional widgets on the Home screen that are the same size as the current one.

- Remove: Hit the Remove button to get rid of a widget on the Home screen.

- Settings: Change how the home screen widgets look.

- App info: Hold the widget you wish to get more information about and then hit the App info icon.

Status bar

There are symbols for your status and notifications in the status bar, so you can see them immediately. In the status bar, you may see the icons listed below.

Status icons

Notification icons

NOTE: You may change the status bar by going to Quick Settings, then selecting More > Status.

Notification panel

You can access settings, notifications, and more from the notification panel.

Quick settings

Notification cards

Device settings

View the notification panel

The notifications panel may be accessed by swiping down.

1. Swipe down from the top screen to get the page with the notification panel.

- To view a specific notice, click on it

- To delete a notice, just drag it to the left or right of the panel.

- In the Notification panel, choose Clear to remove all notifications.

- Click on Notification settings to make changes to a specific notification.

2. Press the ⟨Back button to exit the page of the Notification panel.

Chapter Two
Biometrics and security

This feature allows you to securely sign in to accounts and unlock your phone.

Face recognition

To have your phone unlock itself whenever you glance at it, enable this function.

Take note that this function cannot be accessed until you have established a PIN, Password, or Pattern.

Why When compared to facial recognition, using a pattern, PIN, or password to unlock your smartphone is more secure.

- Unlocking your smartphone is as simple as looking like you.

- Factors that might impact face recognition include: wearing spectacles, thick makeup, beards, or hats.

- Position your face against a brightly light background and make sure your camera lens is clean.

1. Launch the Settings app, go to ⬤ Privacy & Security, then choose Biometrics. Finally, tap on Face recognition.

2. To enroll your face, instructions will show on the screen.

Face recognition management

o Go into your settings, then choose ⬤ Security and privacy, followed by Biometrics, and finally, face recognition.

- It is possible to remove the current face data.

- Enhance the efficiency of the face recognition by including an optional appearance.

- You have the option to disable the facial recognition security.

- To make your face visible in low light, briefly turn up the screen's brightness.

Fingerprint scanner

Another security feature that lets you unlock the smartphone and login in to your Samsung account is fingerprint validation.

Make sure you've set up a password, PIN, or Pattern on your device before you can use this function.

1. To enable face recognition, go to the settings page, hit Security and privacy, then biometrics.

2. To enroll your fingerprint, follow the on-screen instructions.

Fingerprint management

○ Navigate to Security and privacy > Biometrics in the settings menu, and then hit the Fingerprints option. The following choices are at your disposal:

• Pick a fingerprint to edit its name or remove it.

• Pick Add fingerprint if you'd want to add an additional fingerprint. On the screen, you'll see instructions that will show you how to add a fingerprint.

• Verify full registration by scanning a fingerprint.

Biometric settings

○ Go to the settings page, then click on ⬜ Security and privacy, and finally, Biometrics.

● You have the option to display a transition effect when you unlock your smartphone with biometrics.

Mobile Continuity

Your device's storage may be accessed on another computer or mobile device with the help of mobile continuity.

Calls and texts on other devices

You may use your Galaxy mobile to make and receive calls and send and receive SMS messages once you log in to your Samsung account.

1. Press Connected devices > Call & text on other devices in Settings.

2. Hit the button to activate this function.

3. Launch the Samsung account login page on your Galaxy smartphone.

Multi Window

Execute many applications in parallel to multitask. It is possible to use a split screen with apps that allow for multiple windows. Apps may have their windows resized and resized to your liking.

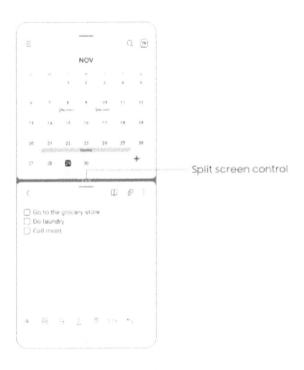

Split screen control

1. Just click the " |||Recent" button on any screen.

2. To launch an app in the split-screen mode, tap its icon.

3. Pick an app in a separate window to bring it into the split-screen mode.

- Drag the margin to resize the window.

Windows control

When using split-screen mode, this functionality changes how program windows are shown.

1. Simply drag the margin in the center of the window to resize the app window.

2. Pressing down in the middle of the window's margin will bring up the following options:

- Toggling between two windows is as simple as touching the ⇅ icon.

- You may add a shortcut to an app pair to either the Apps panel or the Edge panel by touching the ⊞ icon.

Edge panels

View sports and news on the edges of the screen while accessing applications, contacts, tasks, and the news through the Edge panels.

In order to activate the edge panel, you must perform the following:

o Choose Display > Edge panels on the Settings page, then tap the button to enable the function.

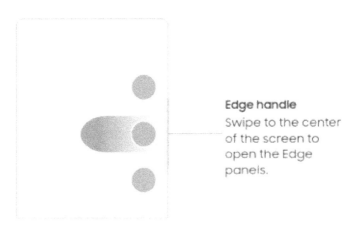

Edge handle
Swipe to the center of the screen to open the Edge panels.

Apps panel

There are two columns on the apps panel where applications may be added.

1. Move the edge handle to the screen's center. When the Apps panel appears, keep swiping.

2. Pick an app to open it. For a comprehensive list of apps, click ⠿ All apps.

In order to set up the Apps bar:

1. To access the Apps panel, drag the Edge panel to the screen's center and swipe it to reveal it.

2. Go to the Apps panel and click the ✎ icon to edit other applications.

• To add an app, simply drag its icon to a blank spot in the Apps panel.

• The order of the apps on the Apps panel is customizable.

• Choose ▬ Remove to remove an app from the applications panel.

3. By clicking the ‹ Back button, you may save your changes.

Configure edge panels

Modifying the Edge panels requires the following steps.

1. Navigate to Panels from the ⚙ Display menu in the Settings app.

2. The following choices are at your disposal:

- ✓ You have the option to enable or disable the Edge panel using the checkbox.

- You have the option to personalize each panel.

- 🔍 To locate panels, use the search bar.

- ⋮ Additional options:

  − Drag panels to reorganize their placement.

  − You may remove installed panels from your device by using the "Uninstall" feature.

  − Put panels out of sight on the lock screen.

- The Galaxy Store: Additional edge panels may be downloaded from there.

Enter texts

On the Keyboard, you have the option to either type or speak the text.

Expand toolbar

Toolbars

You can find the Translator, Clipboard, Emoji, and Stickers on the toolbar.

- o To get the following option, go to the Keyboard and click on ⁎ ⁎ ⁎ Expand Toolbar.

Expression: Explore different types of emojis, GIFs, create custom combined emojis, and more.

Clipboard: Access the clipboard.

One-handed keyboard: Switch to a layout for one-handed use.

Voice Input: Use Samsung voice input.

Settings: Access keyboard settings.

Split keyboard: Change the keyboard to a split version that is separated.

Floating keyboard: Change the keyboard to a floating version that can be moved anywhere on the screen.

Search: Locate specific words or phrases in your conversations.

Translate: Type words or sentences in the keyboard to translate them into another language.

Grammarly: Get suggestions from Grammarly as you type.

Emojis: Insert an emoji.

GIFs: Add animated GIFs.

Bitmoji: Create your own personal emoji and use it in stickers.

Mojitok: Create your own stickers or insert automatically suggested ones.

AR Emoji: Create your own personal emoji and use it in stickers you can share.

Keyboard size: Adjust the height and width of the keyboard.

Text editing: Use an editing panel to help pinpoint text that you want to cut, copy, and paste.

Configure the Samsung keyboard

The keyboard's settings are modifiable.

o   Pressing the ⚙️ Settings key on the keyboard will bring up the choices shown below:

•   Types and languages: Pick the one you like most, along with the keyboard layout.

Smart typing

- With predictive text enabled, suggested words and phrases will pop up as you type on the Samsung keyboard.

- Emoji suggestions: With predictive text enabled, emojis will be recommended to you as you type.

- With auto-replace, you may have predictive text suggestions substitute for what you input.

- Suggest text corrections: When used, this function will automatically check for misspelled words and highlight them in red.

Style and layout

- Samsung keyboard toolbar: You have the option to hide the Samsung keyboard toolbar.

- Elevate the contrast level between the keyboard's keys and background using the high contrast keyboard.

Predictive texts

- Mode: The keyboard may be positioned in either Portrait or Landscape mode.

- You may change the size and transparency of the Samsung keyboard to your liking.

- Layout: Display keyboard shortcuts and special characters.

- Adjust the text size by dragging the slider.

Other settings

- Voice input: Adjust the parameters for voice input.

- Revert to default settings: This option will return you to the initial keyboard configuration and erase any data that has been customized.

Chapter Three
Camera and Gallery

The Camera app lets you take pictures and record movies, and then you can access and modify them in the Gallery.

 Camera

You may achieve professional-quality results with a wide variety of video modes, settings, and lenses.

o   Get the  Camera app started.

TIP: The camera may be activated by pressing the Side key twice from the lock screen.

Settings

Zoom

Shooting modes

Switch cameras

Gallery

Capture

Navigate the camera screen

Make the most of your device's dual-lens camera system; it can capture breathtaking photos.

1. Find the  Camera app on the Apps panel, then adjust your settings so that your photos take use of the following features:

    -   Press and hold the screen area you wish to center the camera on.

- If the screen of the camera is touched, a brightness scale will be shown. To change the camera's exposure, just drag the displaying slider.

• To access the typeface or the back camera, simply slide up or down on the camera screen.

• Swiping left or right on the screen of the camera changes the shooting mode.

• Go to the ⚙ Settings menu to adjust the camera's parameters.

2. Click ◯ to capture a picture.

Configure shooting mode

Either manually choose a shooting mode or let the camera choose the one that would produce the best results for your photos.

○ The camera's screen may be swung to the right or left to switch shooting modes manually.

• When you're shooting portraits, you have the option to change the backdrop.

53

- Photo: Let the camera app choose the best settings for taking pictures.

- Video: Forget about fiddling with the camera app to get the settings just right for filming videos.

- Additionally, you have the option to pick among additional shooting modes. To access the shooting modes tray, which is situated at the bottom of the Camera app screen, users may drag and drop different modes by touching the ⊕ Add button on the screen.

- Decorating an existing photo is possible using the camera feature.

- If you want to take images, you may choose the ISO sensitivity, exposure, white balance, and color tone.

- Create a linear picture by capturing photographs in either a horizontal or vertical direction (panoramic).

- Images that highlight the vibrant colors of food can be captured when this mode is turned on.

– Macro: Images that are three to five centimeters distant from you can be captured.

Record videos

Use your phone's camera to capture what's happening around you while it's happening.

1. Swipe left or right on the Camera screen to switch between shooting modes.

2. To begin filming an already-in-progress event, simply choose Record.

• You may easily snap a screenshot from your video as it's recording by tapping the " Capture" icon.

• Pausing your recording is as easy as clicking the pause button; to continue where you left off, just click the Record icon again.

3. Just hit the Stop button to put the camera to stop recording.

Camera settings

After you complete the instructions below, the camera settings will be preset.

- o To access the following menu items, touch the

  Settings icon on the Camera screen:

Pictures

- You can generate a GIF and take many photos at once by dragging the shutter button to the edge of the screen.

- If you want to save the space on your mobile device to a minimum, you should store photographs in the HEIF format.

- Previewing selfies before saving them allows you to keep them exactly as they seem, without having to flip or otherwise destroy them.

Videos

- High efficiency video format: Using the HEVC format to record videos will help you manage and conserve the capacity on your mobile device.

Some sharing sites might not be compatible with this format for playing back videos.

Useful features

- You can get information out of your images' dark or light spots with the help of the Auto HDR function.

- To help you compose your images and films, you may enable grid lines in the display's view finder.

- You may also add a GPS position tag to your photos or videos to make them easier to monitor.

- Modes of shooting:

– You can regulate the system sound volume, take pictures, capture movies, zoom in and out, and adjust the volume of your media player—all with the touch of a single key.

– You may customize your camera app by adding a floating shutter button that you can position anywhere on the screen.

– Extend your hand with the palm toward the camera lens to speed up the photo taking process.

- Preferences to be saved: When you start up the camera, you have the option to save the last shooting mode, selfie angle, and filter applied.

- Save file to: Select an area on your device to keep the file.

- Watermark: In the lower left corner of the screen, you may apply watermarks to your images.

- Make a sound when you hit the shutter button by adjusting the sound in your camera's settings.

- Reset settings: Return the camera to its initial configuration by going into the camera's settings.

Gallery

The Gallery is where you can organize and modify all of your media files.

- ○ From the App screen, launch the 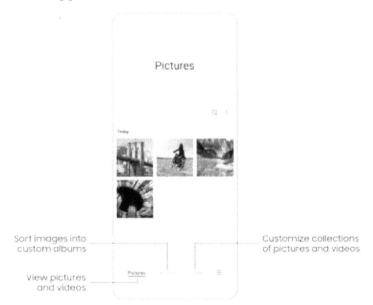Gallery application.

View pictures

The Gallery app allows you to view all of the pictures saved on your smartphone.

1. Press Gallery on the screen of the app.
2. Select the image you wish to see by clicking on it.

- To save your favorite photo, click the " ♡ Add to Favorites" button.

- Additional features may be accessed by pressing the " ⚬ More" tab.

- Information: You will be able to see and change the photo's details.

- Copy to clipboard: Any text or picture that you copy and paste will be saved to the clipboard.

- "Set as wallpaper" means to use the image as a background for your computer.

- Make a connection between your computer and a printer, and then submit the image to print.

Edit pictures

Improve your photos by using the tools provided in the Gallery.

1. Choose Images from the app's ✻ Gallery.

2. Simply tap ✎ on an image to make edits.

- ⬚ Transform: You may easily change the picture's look by rotating, flipping, cropping, or applying other alterations.

- ⊙ Choose a filter to apply a color effect.

- ○ Tone: Control the brightness, contrast, and exposure by clicking the tone button.

- ☺ Text, hand-drawn content, or stickers can be used as decorations.

3. Get it back: Put the original images back.

Play video

Videos on your smartphone may be viewed, favorite, and detailed.

1. Select an image using the �Gallery app.

2. You may watch videos by tapping on them and swiping left or right.

- With the ♡ Add to favorites option, you may save your favorite video to your favorites list.

- By clicking on More, you'll be able to access the following feature:
- Information about the video may be seen and updated in the details section.
- Choose as background: Choose the video and set it as your lock screen wallpaper.

3. Press Play to play the video in your Gallery app.

Edit video

Follow these steps to make changes to the video in your phone's Gallery app.

1. Locate the "Pictures" option in the Gallery.
2. To access it, choose the video you wish to modify.
3. To trim parts, go to the video menu and choose Edit.
4. Choose Save and Confirm when you've finished modifying the video.

Share pictures and videos

Any and all social media sites, including WhatsApp, Facebook, Instagram, Twitter, and TikTok, allow you to

63

easily share your movies and photos with friends and family.

1. Popular Images from the ✳ Gallery app.

2. Select the media file you wish to send by pressing ⋮ More > Edit.

3. Select a sharing app or network by clicking ⌁ Share.

Delete pictures and videos

Removing media files from your smartphone is a simple process.

1. After opening the ✳ Gallery app, choose More > Edit.

2. Select media by pressing on images and videos.

3. Pick out the media files you want to remove, and then hit the 🗑 Delete button.

Screenshot

This function allows you to take a picture of your screen, and then your phone will automatically add it to an album in the gallery app.

o   Take a screenshot by pressing the side and volume down keys at the same time.

Screenshot settings

Adjust your screenshot's parameters.

1. To take a screenshot in the settings app, go to Advanced > Screenshots.

- Show toolbar after capturing: After taking a screenshot, you may see more options on the toolbar.

- Remove after sharing: After sharing a screenshot using the toolbar, you have the option to remove it.

- You may configure your mobile device to conceal the status bar and navigation bar when taking a screenshot.

- Choose between JPG and PNG as the format to store screen captures.

Chapter Four
Apps

You can view all of your downloaded apps from the Apps screen. Their placement on the Home screen is customizable.

- o Unlocked device users may access all apps on the Apps screen by swiping up from the Home screen.

Uninstall or disable apps

You can remove apps that you've downloaded from the Play Store or the Galaxy store. You can just disable the preinstalled application.

- o To access the Apps screen, swipe up from the Home screen. Press and hold an app. From the menu that appears, choose Uninstall or Disable.

Search for apps

If you are having trouble locating certain settings or applications on your mobile device, you may use the search function to discover them.

1. To access the Apps screen, swipe up from the Home screen. Then, type in a term into the search

field. Even as you type in your search terms, relevant apps and settings will start to appear.

2. Just click on the app or setting if it's there.

NOTE: To change your search preferences, go to the More options box and then pick Settings.

Sort apps

You may rearrange the applications and their shortcuts on the applications screen.

- o To access the following arrangement choices, swipe up from the Home screen to see the Apps panel. Then, touch More options and then tap Sort.

- • Manually organize apps in a way that suits you best.

- • The default organization options group apps alphabetically, but you may change it if you like.

NOTE: To eliminate empty space from applications that have been manually placed on the applications screen, go to More options and then pick Clean up pages.

Create a use folders

You may organize and have quick access to your folders on the Apps or Home screens.

1. Unlock your smartphone and slide up from the Home screen to reach the Apps screen. To access an app's shortcut, press and hold its icon until it's highlighted, and then drag it to the top of another app.

2. Launching the program you stacked on top of another will cause the folder to be generated automatically.

*   Name of the folder: Give the folder a name.

*   Select a hue for the folder from the palette.

*   Add apps: A plus sign (+) appears in each folder; tapping it will allow you to choose an app to add to yours. After you're done, touch Done.

3. Please click the Back button to exit the folder.

Copy a folder to a Home screen

You may move a folder to the home screen by following these steps:

o To add an app to your home screen, unlock your mobile phone, slide up from the Home screen to enter the Apps screen, press and hold the app you wish to add, and then select ⊕ Add to Home.

Delete a folder

All of your app shortcuts will still be there on your device, but they will reappear on the Apps screen if you remove a folder from the Home screen or the Apps screen.

1. Press and hold the folder you wish to remove in the Apps list to delete it.

2. To confirm the deletion of a folder, press its icon and then hit the 🗑 Delete folder button.

Apps settings

You have control over the applications that are either installed on your smartphone or those that are available by default.

1. Launch your mobile device's Settings app.

2. Choose the " ⚙ Apps" option.

3. To modify, choose an option:

- You may choose the default app for sending messages, accessing the web, making calls, and more.

- App Settings for Samsung: Select an app from the list of Samsung apps and adjust its settings to your liking.

- Your applications: Pick an app to see and change its settings about privacy and use.

HINT: Pick More choices, and then choose Reset applications, to clear all of your app preferences.

Chapter Five

Contacts

The Contacts app allows you to manage your device's contacts, including creating, editing, deleting, and storing them.

Create a contact

1. Pick Contacts from the Apps screen to add a new contact.

2. Choose the option to create a contact.

3. Please fill out the form for the new contact.

71

4. Choose the option to save it.

Edit a contact

1. Just tap on a contact in the Contacts app to make changes to them.

2. Choose the Edit menu item.

3. To edit or remove data, choose any field.

4. Save your changes when you're done.

Favorite

The Contacts list makes it easy to reach your favorite contacts by grouping them at the top of the list.

1. To open the Contacts app, unlock your device and slide up from the Home screen to get to the Apps panel.

2. To add a contact to your favorites, just touch on their name.

• To delete a contact from your favorites list, simply touch on their name in the list.

Share a contact

1. To share your contacts with others, unlock your device, slide up from the Home screen to see the Apps, then pick the Contacts app. After that, choose a contact to share.

2. On the number you wish to share, find the Share icon and click on it.

3. You have the option to distribute it as a Text or File.

4. After that, decide how you'd like to share the contacts and adhere to the on-screen prompts.

TIP: Hit the QR code scanner after selecting More choices to quickly share a contact's details with others while reading it.

Groups

Using a group, put together contact.

Create a group

1. To arrange your contacts into groups, open your phone and swipe up from the Home screen to

access the Apps screen. From there, select the

Contacts app, and finally, hit the ≡ Open drawer symbol, followed by Groups.

2. If you want to start a new group, just click the "Create group" button.

3. Choose a field below to input the details of the group:

- Give your new group a name so it's easier to find in the Contacts app.

- Making a ringtone for the whole group is step one.

- Add contacts to the newly formed group by clicking the "Add Members" button.

- After completing the steps, click "done."

4. For the modifications to be saved, choose the "Save" option.

Add or remove group contacts

- To add or delete members from a group, open the Contacts app, go to the Groups menu, and tap ≡ on a group.

- Pressing and holding a contact to select it, then tapping the ⬛ Remove symbol, will remove it from a group.

- When you're ready to add a contact to the group, click the ✏ Edit icon and then tap Add member.

- After making the necessary changes, such as adding or deleting contacts from the group, click Save.

Send message to a group

1. Unlock your phone, slide up from the Home screen to display the Apps screen, tap the ⬤ Contacts app, tap ⬛, and then choose "Groups" to send a message to all members of a group at once.

2. To initiate the transmission, go to the " More options" menu and then click "Send message."

Email group members

1. To begin emailing a group, unlock your phone and launch the 👤 Contacts app. From there ☰ , choose a group by touching the "Groups" option.

2. Pick ⋮ More choices and then hit Send email to send the email.

3. After making your selection, click the "Done" button to save the contacts.

- Only members of the group who have provided an email address will be able to see this message.

4. Select an email address and then proceed with the on-screen instructions.

Delete a group

1. Accessing the default 👤 Contacts app on your smartphone is the first step in creating a group. From there, you may remove an existing group by selecting it from the ☰ Open drawer menu and then tapping Groups.

2. Pick More alternatives and then Delete after you've chosen the group.

- Choose Delete group only if you just want to dump that particular group.

- By selecting Delete group and members, you may erase not only the group but also its members.

Merge contacts

1. From the Home screen or the Apps screen, navigate to the Contacts app. From there, choose Open drawer > Manage contacts to combine several contacts with the same identity into one entry.

2. Then, choose Merge contacts. People who have the same name, phone number, and email address will be combined into one contact.

3. After selecting the contacts, click on Merge.

Delete duplicate contacts

You can remove contacts from your smartphone that have multiple identities.

1. To manage your contacts, open the 👤 Contacts app from your device's Apps screen. From there, click ▤ Open drawer > Manage contacts.

2. Choose the option to Remove Duplicate Contacts. View the list of contacts that are similar to this one.

3. To remove specific contacts, just press on their names and then tap the Delete button.

Import contacts

1. From the Home screen, slide up to access the Apps screen. From there, pick 👤 Contacts. Then, click the icon for ▤ Open drawer > Manage contacts to import your contacts as a vCard file (VCF) to your smartphone.

2. Take note of the "Import" or "Export" contact.

3. Pick "Import" from the main menu, then just follow the on-screen instructions.

Export contacts

Your phone's contact list may be exported to vCard format (VCF).

1. To export your phone's contacts to a vCard file, go to your device's home screen, slide up to open the Contacts app from the apps screen, and then tap on " Open drawer" or "Manage contacts" within the contacts app.

2. Find and click the "Import" or "Export" button.

3. Pick "Export" from the main menu, and then just follow the on-screen instructions.

Sync contacts

1. A simple start of the Contacts app, followed by the option to " Open drawer" and then "Manage contacts," will ensure that all of your contacts are current across all of your accounts and devices.

2. Choose "Sync contacts" from the menu.

Delete contacts

To remove one or more contacts, follow these steps.

1. Quickly and easily remove contacts from your smartphone by opening the Contacts app

from the Home or Apps screen, then pressing and holding a contact to select it for deletion.

2. Click 🗑 Delete to proceed with the simple steps to remove the specified contact or contacts.

Chapter Six

 Internet

When you want a fast, safe, and dependable internet app, go no further than Samsung. Secret Mode, Biometric Web Login, and Content Blocker are additional tools that can help you navigate the web safely.

Browser tabs

You may see numerous websites simultaneously using the browser tabs.

○ After starting up your mobile device's  Web browser, go to the Apps menu, and then select New tab from the Tabs menu to start a new tab.

81

- Select Close tab from the Tabs menu to close all open tabs.

Create a bookmark

○ After you unlock your smartphone, open the Internet app from the Home or Apps screen.

Then, click the icon that says " Add to bookmarks" to store the launch webpage. This way, you can easily access apps that you use often.

Open a Bookmark

1. Pressing the Bookmarks button in the Internet app will take you to the bookmarked page.

2. Choose a page from your collection of bookmarked websites.

Save a webpage

○ The Internet app does not come with many choices for saving webpages; nevertheless, you may get these options by going to ░░░Tools > Add page.

- Bookmarks: Save a page as a favorite in the internet app.

- Convenient access: The Internet app allows you to see a list of the websites that you visit frequently.

- One useful feature of the internet app is the ability to add a shortcut to a website on the home screen.

- You may store webpage content to your Smartphone using the internet app. This way, you can see it offline.

View history

○ In the ◯ Internet app, you may view your browser history by going to the ░░░Tools menu.

TIP: By selecting ░More options and choosing Clear History, you may erase all traces of your web usage.

Share pages

Your web pages can be shared with your connections.

o Navigate to the ⬤ Internet app, hit the ☰ Tools icon, and then choose Share. Then, follow the simple steps to share web pages with your friends, family, and other social media platforms.

Secret mode

Because they are not saved in your browser's or search history, websites visited in hidden mode cannot leave any digital footprints. When you're surfing, the hidden tab is likewise darker than the regular tab.

Your downloaded files will remain accessible on your device even after you exit the secret mode menu.

1. Start the ⬤ Internet app, go to the ☐ Tabs menu, and finally, press Turn on hidden mode to activate the feature.

2. Press the Start button to begin browsing in hidden mode.

Secret mode settings

Passwords or biometric locks are necessary for the secret mode functionality to function properly.

1. Unlock your mobile device, launch the Internet app, and then select Tabs to begin setting this up.

2. By tapping the More options button and then selecting Secret mode settings, you will be able to access the following option:

- Make use of a password: Make sure the password you choose for secret mode is highly robust.

- Facial recognition: Turning it on will allow you to hide your secret mode.

- Fingerprints: The secret mode can be protected by setting up a fingerprint.

- Reset to secret mode: This is where you may erase all of your secret mode data and put it back to its factory settings.

Turn off secret mode

Follow these steps to exit hidden mode and return to the Internet app's regular surfing mode:

○ After starting the ⬤ Internet app, go to ⬜ Tabs and then touch on Switch off hidden mode.

Messages

"Messages" is an app that lets you instantly greet friends and family, initiate conversations, make calls, block numbers, and exchange photographs.

○ To open the 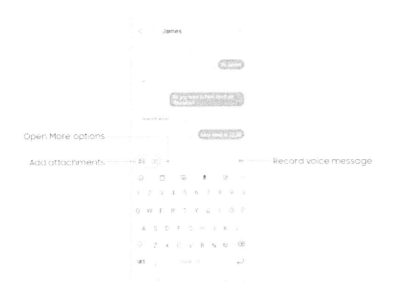 Messages app on your phone, unlock it, and then slide up from the Home screen to expose the Apps screen. If the Messages icon isn't already there, swipe it to the right.

Then, click the symbol and choose Compose to start writing a new message.

Message search

If you have misplaced a message and don't know where to look, you may use the app's search function to locate it.

1. Press the ⌕ Search icon that appears when you open the 💬 Messages app on your smartphone.

2. Just type in the word(s) you want to find and hit the ⌕ Search button.

Delete conversation

Upon deletion, conversations will no longer be visible in the conversation history.

1. On the screen of the 💬 Messages app, tap the ⋮ More option button, and then choose Delete.

2. To erase messages, just pick them.

3. To erase all of the messages, hit 🗑 Erase all. Then, follow the onscreen instructions.

Send SOS message

This function allows you to send messages indicating your position to emergency numbers, so there's no need to worry when you're in a dire situation.

1. To enable this option in the Settings app, go to the Advanced features section, then press on Send SOS message. Finally, hit ⬛ On.

- The SOS message may be sent by pressing the side key three or four times, respectively.

- In order to choose a contact to contact following the transmission of an SOS message, choose Auto call someone.

- Pick "Attach image" to include photos taken by either your front or back camera.

- Choose "Attach audio recording" if you would want to include a brief audio clip with your words.

- Press the Send message button to import your phone's contact list or to add a new contact.

2. Three or four presses of the side key will deliver the message.

Message settings

You may modify the settings for multimedia messages or set them up in the following ways.

○ To configure message settings, go to Messages, click the More option button, and then choose Settings.

Emergency alerts

Enabling this function on your mobile device will notify you of any potential dangers that may approach your device. An emergency communication can be received at no cost.

1. Navigate to the Settings menu, then choose Notification, and finally, Advanced settings to enable this.

2. To modify the notice for emergency alerts, choose Wireless Emergency Alerts.

My Files

You may access all of the files—pictures, movies, music, and more—stored on your mobile device using the My Files app. All of the data on your SD card or in your cloud storage accounts may be accessed and managed via this program.

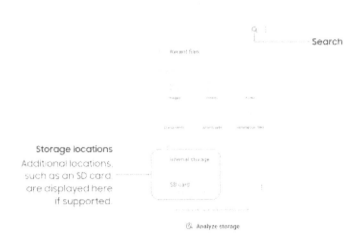

File groups

Navigate to the following folders to view the files saved on your device:

- Files you have recently opened: This is where you can see all of the files you have lately opened.

- Categories: Here you may sort files by kind.

- Files saved on your phone, on the cloud, or on an SD card may all be accessed from this section.

- Cloud accounts differ based on the service you log in to.

- Analyze your storage space: This is where you can find out what's eating up all that room.

My File settings

The My Files menu allows you to do a lot more, such edit, delete, and search for files.

o The following options may be accessed using the My Files app:

- Search: This function allows you to locate a certain file or folder.

- Additional options:

- The first is a cloud service, which mobile device may connect to

- To find out what's using up all your storage space, you need do an analysis of your storage
- The trash can is where you may permanently remove files from your mobile device.
- Settings: This is where you may access the app's settings.

Chapter Seven

Phone

The Phone app allows users to make, receive, refuse, and send calls to voicemail. Viewing recent calls and preferred contacts is also possible via the phone app.

Calls

The Phone app allows users to make, receive, and reject calls from any screen.

Make a call

Follow these steps while talking on the phone to make a call.

- Hit ⊙ Call after entering the number you wish to call using the keyboard in the ⊙ Phone app.

Make a call from Recent

Use your recent calls list to make a call.

- Go to the ⊙ Phone app, find the number you wish to contact in your recent call list, and then tap the ⊙ Contact option.

Make a call from contacts

If you have the Contacts app on your smartphone, you may make calls by following these steps.

- From the ⊙ Contacts app, swipe your finger right over the contact you wish to call.

Answer a call

As soon as a call reaches your phone, you'll hear a tone and see the caller ID displayed on your screen.

o   On the incoming call screen, you may choose to

     answer calls by dragging the Answer button to

     the right side of the screen.

Decline a call

o   Simply slide the Reject button to the left side

     of the screen to send incoming calls to voicemail

     or reject them altogether.

Decline with a message

If you are unable to answer an incoming call due to being

busy or in the wrong place, you can utilize the steps

outlined below to send a text message declining the call.

o   To pick a message to send to the individual, drag

     the Send message option upward and click on it.

End a call

You have the option to stop a call whenever you're

through speaking. To stop a continuing call, do the

indicated action below.

o   After a call is active, you can end it by clicking the

"⬤ End" button.

Actions while on a call

It is possible to multitask while on a call, doing things like adjusting the volume or pairing a Bluetooth headset with your main device. Follow the steps shown below to adjust the call volume:

o   To adjust the level of loudness, press the Up or Down volume buttons, respectively.

Switch to headset or speaker

You may answer calls using an external hearing aid, such as a Bluetooth headset, on the device you're now using. If you want to use the device's main speaker or Bluetooth headset to answer a call, follow these steps.

o   To listen to a caller through the speaker, press the

🔊 Speaker button. To listen using a Bluetooth

headset, click the Bluetooth button.

Multitask

The status bar of your phone will display the live call even if you leave the screen of the ongoing call to utilize another app on your device.

If you want to get back to the call screen, do this:

o Touch the call by dragging the status bar lower.

To hang up a call while you're multitasking, follow these steps:

o To see which call is now active, drag the Status bar to the bottom of the screen and then click the End call button.

Call background

You may change the backdrop while a call is in progress. Here are the steps you need to follow to do this:

o After you've logged in, slide up from the bottom of the Home screen to get the Apps screen. From there, pick the Phone app. From the More options menu, go to Settings, and finally, choose Call background:

- Preferences: Choose the layout for the caller's information, including any profile pictures associated to the contact.

- Background: During a conversation, you may select a background from your photo library and apply it to your applications.

Call pop-up settings

No matter what else you're doing, any incoming call will show up as a pop-up window.

- Go to the Home screen menu, open the Phone app, and from there, choose More options, Settings, and Call display when using applications.

- When a call comes in, you may choose to see it on the full screen.

- The first option is "pop-up," which will cause a window to display on top of your screen whenever you get a call.

- One option is to have a tiny pop-up window display whenever a call comes in.

- When you activate this feature, all calls that you answer will stay in the pop-up window.

Manage calls

You may control call actions, block numbers, create fast dials, and set up voicemail from the call logs, where all your calls are logged.

Call logs

No call goes unrecorded here, whether it's answered, missed, or dialed.

- Go to the Phone app, then select "Recent" to view all of the calls that have been made recently in the Call log. The caller's identity will be recorded in the call log even if you don't have the number saved in your contact list.

Save a contact from recent

Any calls you make can be preserved in your recent calls log.

1. In the Phone app, choose the "Recent" option.

2. In order to add a call's details to your contact list, find the call you wish to add and click the "Add to contact" button.

3. You may choose "Update existing contacts" or "Create new contact" after tapping a profile.

Delete call records

Follow these steps to remove a single contact or clean your whole call history:

1. Find the "Recent" option in the Phone app's menu and choose it.

2. Find the call you wish to remove and hold down the button.

3. To confirm the deletion, click the Delete icon.

Block a number

Once you've blocked a number, you won't get any further calls or messages from that number. If they try to call, you'll be able to refuse and send them to voicemail.

1. From the Phone menu, choose the "Recent" option.

2. You may block a specific contact by selecting them.

3. Confirm the action by clicking ⊙ Details > ⊘ Block when you see the number.

TIP: If you want to block a contact from the phone as well, go to More options > Settings > Block numbers.

Speed dial

The steps below will show you how to give a contact a speed dial number.

1. Step by step instructions for setting a speed dial number: open the ⓒ Phone app, go to Keypad, then More options, and lastly, choose Speed dial numbers. The speed dial screen will display all of the reserved speed dial numbers.

2. Choose a number that is not associated with any specific person or company.

• You may use the ▽ Menu icon to choose a number that isn't in the sequence.

• The "1" number is designated for voicemail at all times.

3. Click ▲Add from Contacts or input the contact's information to provide a number.

- You will see the contacts you have chosen in the speed dial box.

Make a call with speed dial

Speed dial numbers can be used to make calls.

○ Open the Ⓒ Phone app. Then, quickly dial the desired number by pressing and holding.

- Simply input the first digit of the speed dial number and then press and hold the last digit if the number is more than one digit.

Remove a speed dial number

Following these steps will delete the allocated number from the contact record.

1. Choose "Speed dial" from the Ⓒ Phone app's More options menu.

2. To remove the speed dial number, click the Delete symbol that appears next to the contact.

103

Emergency calls

Even with a deactivated smartphone, you can still make an emergency call.

○ To initiate an emergency call, launch the 📞 Phone app, then input the regional emergency number, and last, tap on Call.

TIP: You can still dial emergency numbers even while your screen is locked.

Phone settings

From the Phone settings, you can adjust all the parameters linked to your Phone app.

○ From the home or Apps screen, launch the 📞 Phone app. Then, tap ⋮ More options to adjust the settings.

Optional calling services

Depending on your phone carrier and plan, your device may be able to make calls to the numbers shown below.

Place a multiparty call

From this option, you may initiate a conference call.

1. While one call is in progress, you can initiate a second one by clicking the " Add call" icon.

2. Once the second call has been returned:

- To switch between calls, just hit the Swap button.

- Press Merge to simultaneously listen to both calls.

Video calls

Get a video chat going:

o Open the Phone app on your device and go to the Video Calls menu (, ,)to start a video call.

Real Time Text (RTT)

You can use the RTT calling capability to call devices that support it or that are linked to a teletypewriter (TTY). The RTT symbol will be shown if an RTT call is received.

1. Navigate to the Phone app's Settings by tapping the More option.

2. Click on "Real Time Text."

105

- RTT call button: Set the location where the RTT call button will show.

- Use an external TTY keyboard: By connecting an external keyboard to your device, you can hide the RTT keyboard.

- When prompted, select "TTY mode" for the keyboard you're using.

Samsung Medical

Everyday habits like eating well and exercising regularly may be tracked with the Samsung Health app. To get more details about this app, go to samsung.com/us/support/owners/app/samsung-health.

NOTE: The data gathered from this device is not meant to be used for the purpose of diagnosing, treating, preventing, or curing any illness or infection. Neither Samsung Health nor any associated applications are to be used for this purpose.

Factors like as user-provided information, ambient circumstances, and user-configuration might impact the device's facts.

Before you start exercising

Patients with any of the following medical issues should not begin an exercise program without first consulting their heath care provider or other appropriate medical professional. Activities like brisk walking are generally considered safe for most individuals to practice.

- Conditions affecting the heart, lungs, diabetes, liver, kidneys, and joints, as well as arthritis.
- Aches and pains in the chest, neck, and arm area that worsen with movement;
- Deterioration of Mind;
- Ankle edema, especially at night;
- A dizzy or racing heart;

Settings
Access settings

Depending on your device, there may be a number of methods to access the phone's settings.

- Sliding down the Home screen brings up the notification panel, from which you may choose the ⚙ Settings option.

- Press the ⚙ Settings button on the Apps screen to open the Settings menu.

Search for Settings

When you utilize the search tool on your smartphone, you can find and see the settings.

1. Just open the Settings app and use the 🔍 Search button to find the applications or settings.

2. To access the configuration, choose an outcome.

Chapter Eight
Connections

Your device's connections to other mobile networks can be controlled and monitored.

Wi-Fi

A friend's hotspot or a public internet connection can be accessed using your device's Wi-Fi when Wi-Fi is enabled.

1. To access the Settings menu, swipe up from the Home screen to see the Apps screen. From there, choose the Setting app and navigate to Connections > Wi-Fi. Scan for accessible networks by touching the On symbol after selecting Wi-Fi from the Connections menu.

2. To connect to a network, choose one and, if prompted, enter the password.

Connect to a hidden network

Input the hotspot connection data (Name, password, and security type) if the network you wish to connect is still not shown after a network scan.

1. If you can't find the Settings app on your Home screen, you may reach it by swiping up to the Apps screen and selecting "Settings." From there, go to Connections > Wi-Fi. After that, pick Connection and then Wi-Fi. Finally, touch On to enable Wi-Fi.

2. At the very bottom of the network list, you should see an Add option; click on it.

3. Fill in the details of the network:

   • The exact name of the network must be entered.

   • In the "Security" section, you may choose a level of protection and, if prompted, provide a password.

   • Enhanced features: choices for IP and proxy.

4. After you finish, click the "Save" button.

TIP: If you have a smartphone, you can scan a QR code and then tap the QR scanner symbol to connect to the network.

Advanced Wi-Fi Settings

You may manage stored networks, find your phone's network address, sort connections by kind and source, and access advanced Wi-Fi options from this menu.

1. Swipe up from the Home screen to get to the Apps panel. Open the app, then go to Connections > Wi-Fi. Finally, tap On to turn on Wi-Fi if you can't find the Setting page on the Home screen.

2. Pick Advanced from the " More options" menu.

- Mobile data backup: Once enabled, your phone will automatically switch to mobile data in the event that your Wi-Fi signal is spotty or unstable, and then back to Wi-Fi again if no longer an issue.

- You may program your device to automatically turn on Wi-Fi when you're in an area where you've used it before.

- You will receive a notice from your smartphone as soon as it identifies open networks in its vicinity.

- You can rejoin to or delete previously stored networks using the network administration interface.

- Apps that have recently utilized your Wi-Fi may be found in the Wi-Fi control history.

- Your device has the capability to connect to Hotspot 2.0-compatible hotspots.

- Set up certificates for authentication.

Wi-Fi Direct

This functionality allows for the direct sharing of connections across devices.

1. You may activate Wi-Fi by going to the Settings app, selecting Connection, tapping Wi-Fi, and finally tapping On.

2. Under " More options," find Wi-Fi direct and select it.

3. Just follow the onscreen prompts to connect your device.

113

Disconnect from a Wi-Fi Direct

To disconnect from a Wi-Fi direct connection, follow these steps.

o   You can reach the Settings app from the Home screen or the Apps screen. From there, choose Connection, then Wi-Fi. Next, press on More choices. Finally, tap on Wi-Fi Direct. To detach it, select a device.

Bluetooth

Media items such as photos, videos, music, and documents may be easily shared when your mobile phone is linked to a Bluetooth device. In order for your smartphone to connect with other devices, such as headphones or your car's infotainment system, you must enable Bluetooth.

1.   From the Home screen or the Apps screen, open the settings app. From there, choose Connections. Touch on Bluetooth. Finally, touch On to enable the Bluetooth.

2. Just follow the simple instructions after selecting a device to connect to.

Rename a paired device

Assign a unique name to a gadget so it may be easily identified.

1. You may change the name of a connected device by going into the Settings app, selecting Connection, and finally tapping on Bluetooth.

2. Next to the device, you should see the Settings icon; click on it to alter the name.

3. Click the Rename button once you've entered the name you wish to use for the device.

Unpair from a Bluetooth device

You have to couple the devices again once they've lost connectivity in order to bring them back online.

1. Before you may unpair from a Bluetooth device, make sure that Bluetooth is turned on in the Settings app's Connections menu.

115

2. Select the ⚙ Settings icon that appears next to the name of the device.

Advanced options

The following Bluetooth capabilities can be accessed through the advanced menu.

1. Navigate to the Settings app on your Galaxy A16, then choose 📶 Connections, and finally, touch on Bluetooth.

2. Before you may access the advanced features, choose ⋮ More choices.

- You can sync data sent over Bluetooth with your Samsung account, which allows you to link files with Samsung Cloud.

- Music Share: This is a great tool for sharing music with loved ones on various social networking sites.

- When you connect a Bluetooth device to your phone, you may set it to play a certain ringtone whenever a call comes in.

116

- Applications that have made recent use of Bluetooth will be displayed in the Bluetooth control history.

- Add the device whose pairing request you do not wish to accept here in order to block pairing requests.

NFC and Payments

Make advantage of this function to converse with other people even when you don't have access to the internet. To use this function, your device must be within 4 cm of the supporting device, and the supporting device must also be in range.

o Select Connection in the Settings app, then click NFC and contactless payment. Finally, touch to use this feature.

Tap and Pay

When you use the NFC payment app, all you have to do is hold your phone up to a card reader that is compatible with your device.

1. Choose 📶 Connections in the Settings app, then touch NFC and contactless payments, and finally click 🌙 to accomplish this.

2. Call up the default payment app by tapping the Contactless button.

- Choose a functional app that you can use to make payments.

- To make the payment using another app that is presently open, choose Pay with currently open app.

- Pick the service you desire after selecting other if you'd rather utilize a different payment provider by default.

Airplane Mode

To disable all wireless and data connections, including Bluetooth, calling, texting, Wi-Fi, data, and hotspot, just switch to airplane mode (also known as flight mode) o Go to Settings, then touch on Connections. Then, tap on Airplane mode. Finally, click to activate it.

NOTE: It's possible that using a smartphone while traveling is against the laws of the ship or aircraft.

Mobile networks

You may utilize mobile data and connect to a mobile network with the Samsung Galaxy A16.

o Start by going to the Application screen, then go to Settings. Scroll down until you see Connections, and finally, press on Mobile networks.

• Mobile data: Activate the mobile data feature.

• Data roaming abroad: You have the option to customize data, voice, and text roaming while traveling abroad.

• Enable 2G service: This will let you to use the 2G service in places where cellular coverage is restricted.

- For the "Access Point Names" (APNs), choose them. It contains the necessary network settings for your phone to connect to your carrier.

- Network operators: Pick a network among the ones that are offered.

Data Usage

It is possible to track how much data and Wi-Fi you use. You may also put restrictions on it.

o After accessing the Home or Apps screen on your Galaxy A16, go to Settings. Then, touch on Connections. Lastly, press on Data use.

Turn on Data saver

Turning on data saver mode is a simple way to reduce your data use. It also stops background apps from transferring data.

1. To access data saving, open the settings app, press and hold the Connections icon, then choose data consumption.

2. You may activate data saver by tapping .

- With Data Saver enabled, you may grant some apps unrestricted access to data by tapping the button next to each app.

Monitor mobile data

Limits may be set to control and keep tabs on your mobile data.

o Select Settings from the Home or Apps panel. Then, go to Connections and last, Data use.

- Mobile data: Configure your gadget so that it uses the data allotted to you each month.

- Turning on mobile data services when traveling overseas is an option.

- Apps that only operate with mobile data: You may configure some apps to utilize mobile data even while your smartphone is connected to Wi-Fi.

- Mobile data usage: track the data use over a period of time.

NOTE: You will need to make changes to your monthly plan in order for it to be in sync with your carrier's billing data. Please be aware that this function allows you to track the real data use.

Monitor Wi-Fi data

1. Navigate to the Settings app from the Home or Apps screen, then tap on Connections. From there, tap on Data consumption to monitor Wi-Fi data and set limitations.

2. To see the data use graph, choose Wi-Fi data usage.

Mobile Hotspot

Turning on your mobile hotspot allows you to share your data or internet connection with other devices.

1. To activate Hotspot, open the Settings app, go to Connection > Mobile Hotspot & Tethering > Mobile Hotspot, and finally, tap the activation button.

2. A simple explanation would be to have the other user activate their Wi-Fi, then locate your device and input the password.

TIP: all it takes to scan a QR code with your mobile device is a tap.

Configure Mobile Hotspot Settings

1. Select 🔛Connections in the options app. Then, click Mobile hotspot & tethering. Finally, tap Mobile hotspot to setup your mobile hotspot connection options.

2. When you click "Configure," the following will show up:

- Network name: You can see the name of your hotspot and modify it if you want to.

- Security: Set the degree of protection for your mobile hotspot.

- View your current password and change it to something strong.

- Depending on your needs, you may choose from a variety of bandwidth options.

- Here you may find more advanced options for customizing the hotspot settings.

Auto Hotspot

1. Launch the Settings app from the Home or Apps screen. Then, click 🔛Connections > Mobile

hotspot & tethering > Mobile hotspot. This will allow you to automatically share your mobile hotspot with devices that are logged into your Samsung account.

2. Go ahead and activate Auto Hotspot by tapping .

Tethering

1. Just open the Settings app, choose Connections, and then tap Mobile hotspot & tethering to start sharing your device's internet with a PC using a USB cable.

2. Pick one of these alternatives:

- To link up with the PC with a USB connection, choose USB tethering.

- If you want to use an Ethernet adapter to link up to the PC, choose that option.

Connect to a Printer

1. Go into the Settings app on your mobile device, then tap on Connections. From there, choose More connection settings, and finally, Printing

to connect your phone to a printer. This will make printing files a breeze.

2. Click More settings, then select Default print service, and finally, touch Add printer.

- If your computer requires a plug-in, choose " Download plug-in" and follow the simple steps to establish a print service.

TIP: Not all applications support printing.

Virtual Private Networks

1. In order to establish a VPN connection on your mobile device to a private network, you will need to obtain the necessary connection details from your VPN provider.

   NOTE: Virtual Private Networks (VPN) should be noted.

2. Pick VPN from the list of available Connections in the Settings app that you can access from the Home screen.

3. Choose "Add VPN profile" from the " More options" menu.

4. Type in the VPN credentials that your network administrator has given you.

5. Finally, click "Save" to finish.

Manage a VPN

1. Simply open the Settings app, go to the Connections section, and then choose "More connection settings" before finally selecting VPN.

2. A Setting icon will appear next to the VPN; click on it.

3. Adjust the VPN settings to your liking and hit "Save"

4. Select "Delete" to uninstall the VPN.

Connect to a VPN

Joining a Virtual Private Network may be done by following the steps below.

1. Open your phone's Settings app and go to Connections to set up a virtual private network.

2. Go to "More connection settings" and then choose VPN.

3. After you've chosen your VPN, click "Connect" to establish a connection.

• To unlink from a network, just choose the VPN you wish to unlink from and then hit the "Disconnect" button.

Private DNS

Make sure your phone is set up to connect to a private DNS by following these instructions.

1. Open the Settings app and go to 🔘 Connections to set up your mobile device to connect to a private DNS server.

2. Choose Private DNS from the "More connection settings" menu.

3. Choose an option to establish a private DNS connection.

4. Choose the option to save it.

Ethernet

1. If you're in an area without wireless service, you may connect your phone to a local network using an Ethernet adapter.

2. Go to the Settings app and then choose Connections.

3. Choose "More connection settings," then "Ethernet," and finally, follow the on-screen prompts.

Sound and Vibration

Take charge of the vibration and sound effects that serve as alerts for incoming calls, messages, and other noises.

Sound mode

- Choose a setting under Sounds & vibration in the Settings app to adjust the volume to your hearing needs.

- Sound: If you go into the Sound settings, you can adjust the volume, enable vibrations, and utilize them for alerts and notifications.

- Make your phone vibrate when it rings: Turn on this feature.

- To limit vibration to alerts and notifications exclusively, turn on the "Vibrate" feature.

- Turn off all notifications by muting your smartphone.

- Turn your phone's sound down for a certain amount of time using the temporary mute feature.

Vibrations

1. Find 📢 Sounds & vibration in your phone's Settings menu, and then adjust the timing and intensity of the vibrations.

2. Choose an option to personalize:

- Pick a vibrating pattern for incoming calls if you like.

- Select your preferred notification vibration pattern under the "Notifications" menu.

- Pull the Vibration slider to adjust the level of vibration for calls, taps, and notifications.

Volume

○ Launch the Settings app, then click 📢 Sounds & vibration, and finally, Volume. From there, you can modify the volume level of calls, media, notifications, and system sounds by pulling the sliders for each type of sound.

TIP: You may adjust the volume using the buttons on the side of the device. When you hit the side key, a menu will popup indicating the current volume level of your device. You may adjust the volume by dragging the slider.

Media volume limit

1. Navigate to Settings > Sounds & vibration > Volume to adjust the volume output for your headphones or Bluetooth speaker.

2. Make sure to choose Media Volume limit from the list of More options.

3. To activate the functionality, press .

- Drag the Custom volume limit slider to the desired maximum output level.

  o Click "Set Volume Limit PIN" to assign a temporary PIN that you may use to adjust the volume.

Ringtone

1. Press Sounds & vibration > Ringtone after going into Settings to set a ringtone or import one from your computer.

2. You may preview ringtones that are already installed by tapping on them, or you can add ringtones from your local files by clicking the Add button.

Notification sound

1. Launch Settings, then select Sounds & vibration, and finally touch Notification sound to configure the sound that will play whenever a notification is received.

2. Before you apply a sound, you may hear it briefly play by clicking on it.

System sound and vibration

o Locate the following choices in the System sound/vibration control section of the Settings menu, then select Sounds & vibration. Here you may configure the device to respond to touches and charges with sound and vibration:

Sound

- Touch interactions: your mobile device has the option to record a sound whenever the screen is touched.

- You have the option to configure your mobile device to emit a sound whenever it is locked or unlocked through the screens.

- If your device has a charging alert, it will sound an alarm when a charger is attached.

- When you activate dial pad tones, your phone will make a sound whenever you press the keypad.

- To activate the phone's sound feature when using the Samsung Keyboard, go to Settings > Keyboard.

Vibration

- Have the following activated so that they vibrate when used:

- A vibration alert will go off on your phone whenever one of the navigation keys is pressed.

- Your phone will vibrate when you dial on the keyboard.

- Gestures for navigation: your phone will vibrate when you use a gesture.

- When charging, your smartphone will make a vibrating sound.

- Samsung keyboard: When you type on the Samsung keyboard, your phone will vibrate.

Do Not Disturb

Use the "Do Not Disturb" feature to silence incoming calls and alerts. You may also choose which applications, alerts, and calls to ignore.

- To access the choices for Do Not Disturb, launch the Settings app from either the Home or Apps screen. Then, go to Notifications and then choose "Do not disturb."

- When you turn on "Do not disturb," all incoming calls and notifications will be muted.

- How much time?To manually activate Do Not Disturb, you can establish a timer.

Schedule

- Bedtime: Establish a regular time to turn off all notifications.

- Schedule: Make it a habit to put your phone in Do Not Disturb mode at certain times each day.

Exceptions

- You may enable "Do not disturb" for incoming calls, texts, and chats by tapping the corresponding button.

- While this mode is active, you may enable alerts, vibrations, events, reminders, and more using sound and sound effects.

- Apps: In the Do Not Disturb menu, choose which applications you would like to receive alerts from while in that mode

- Hide notifications: You have the option to do so in the settings.

Alert when phone picked up

If you enable this feature, your phone will vibrate whenever you pick it up to alert you of incoming calls or texts.

- o Locate the Advanced features submenu, then go to Motions & gestures, and finally, pick Alert from the Settings menu.

Turn over to mute

In order to silence any incoming calls, alerts, or texts, turn your smartphone so that it faces the ground.

o Go to the Apps screen, then pick Settings. Then, go to Advanced features, then motions and gestures. Finally, press the button.

Chapter Nine
Display

You may adjust the device's display settings, including the brightness, font size, and timeout delay.

Dark mode

To protect your eyes from staring at your phone all night long, turn on "Dark mode" so you can see better.

- o Launch the Settings app from either the Apps screen or the Home screen. Then, touch on Display to get the display options shown below.

- As a default, your phone will use the light theme.

- One option is to use a dark theme on your mobile device.

- Dark mode settings: Establish a pattern for the application of dark mode and when it should be used.

- – You have the option to configure dark mode to activate at sunrise or sunset.

- – With the adaptive color filter, you can lessen the strain on your eyes when using your smartphone at night. Between the hours of sunset and sunrise, automatically activate the blue light filter.

Screen brightness

Make sure your screen is as bright as your eyes need it to be.

1. Navigate to the   Display section in your smartphone's Settings.
2. You can personalize the following options:

- Using the slider that is given, you may change the brightness.
- To change the screen's brightness depending on the ambient light, use the "Adaptive brightness" option.

TIP: You can still change the brightness level on the Quick Setting menu.

Motion Smoothness

Raising the screen's refresh rate gives you a sample of the silky scrolling and more lifelike animation.

1. When you're in the   Display menu of the Settings app, choose Motion Smoothness.

2. Choose a choice and then hit the Apply button.

Eye comfort shield

After you enable this option, you'll be able to use your smartphone calmly even after the sun goes down. This function may be programmed to activate and deactivate automatically.

- o To access the ⚙ Display menu, unlock your phone and go to the Settings app. From there, touch on Eye Comfort Shield. From the list of options, choose one:

- Go to "Set schedule." From there, you may choose "Always on," "Sunrise," "Sunset," or "Custom" based on your usage habits.

- To change the filter's opacity, use the temperature slider.

Font size and style

You can change the fonts that your Samsung phone uses for typing.

○ You may access the following by going to the Display menu, then selecting "Font size and style" under settings:

• Press the Font style button to change the font.

– Pick a typeface or use the Galaxy Store's Download button.

• When you choose "Bold font," all of the text will be bolded.

• The font size may be adjusted by dragging the slider.

Screen zoom

Adjust the zoom level to make material more readable on your mobile device. To adjust the magnification level, do the following.

1. Start by opening the Settings app. Then, touch on the Display icon. From there, choose Screen zoom.

2. To make your selection, simply drag the slider.

Full screen apps

o Open Settings, then tap ⬡ Display > Full screen applications. From there, choose the program you want to use in full screen mode.

Screen timeout

Your screen may be programmed to automatically turn off after a predetermined period of time. It may be thirty seconds or fifteen, depending on the situation.

o Open the Settings app, then tap the ⬡ Display icon, then choose Screen timeout. From there, you may set a time restriction.

Touch sensitivity

Even with a screen protector, you may speed up the response time to taps by increasing the touch sensitivity.

o Start by opening the Settings app. Then, tap the ⬡ Display icon. Finally, touch sensitivity to enable it.

Screen saver

When your screen is off or your device is charging, you may personalize it with a photo or color that you choose.

1. Simply launch the Settings app, navigate to the Display menu, and finally, hit the Screen saver option.

2. Give some thought to the following choices:

- Choose "None" if you'd rather not display a screen saver.

- Colors: To see a screen with shifting colors, use the selection.

- Picture gallery: Slideshow photos into the Picture gallery.

- Picture frame: Showcase your photographs in the Picture frame.

- Images: Change the way your Google photographs will display your photographs.

3. Press "Preview" to see the chosen image before you apply it to the screen.

TIP: The Settings icon is located next to each function; clicking it will bring up further settings.

Lift to wake

Turn your smartphone on whenever you lift it up by activating this function.

- o To activate the function, launch the Settings app, navigate to Advanced features, and finally, tap on Motions and gestures. From there, choose Lift to wake.

Double tap to turn on screen

Toggle this feature on to enable the ability to double-tap the screen to activate it, bypassing the need to hit the Side key.

- o Launch the Settings app, then navigate to Advanced features, then motions & gestures. Finally, find the option to double-tap the screen to activate it.

Double tap to turn off screen

If you want to be able to power down your smartphone with a double tap on the screen instead of pressing the Side key, you may enable this option.

o To access the   Advanced features, open the Settings app. Then, go to Motions and gestures. Finally, double-tap the screen to turn it off.

Keep screen on while viewing

o Navigate to the Settings app, then select Advanced features, then Motions and gestures, and finally, Keep screen on when viewing. Press the   button to keep the screen on while you view content.

One-handed mode

To make your smartphone one-handed-operable, turn on this function.

1. To access one-handed mode, go to the Settings menu and then touch on   Advanced features.

2. After touching   , you'll see options to enable the function. Choose one:

• The gesture feature may be used by swiping down from the center of the bottom edge of the screen.

- Button: To minimize the screen size, double-tap the ⬜ Home button twice in rapid succession.

Lock screen and security

To keep your smartphone's private features safe, you may set a screen lock.

Screen lock types

Depending on the model, a phone's primary screen lock options can be a PIN, pattern, password, swipe, none, fingerprint, or face recognition.

Set a secure screen lock

Use a "PIN," "Pattern," "Password," or "Biometric lock" to protect your phone and safeguard its contents. When configuring your device, these lock methods are crucial.

1. Launch the Settings app. Then, go to Lock screen > Screen lock type. From there, pick from Pattern, PIN, or Password as your preferred method of screen lock.

2. To have the lock screen display notifications, choose . A list of choices will be displayed:

- Just Icons: Your smartphone may be configured to display notification icons only, without any accompanying text.

- Information: You have the option to display notification information on the Lock screen on your smartphone.

- Notification content kept secret: In the Notification panel, you may disable the display of alerts on your phone.

- Choose which notifications you would want to have shown on the lock screen under the "Notifications to show" section.

3. Click "Done" to close the menu when you're finished.

4. To set up the screen lock, go to the following menu:

- You may program your phone to unlock automatically when it detects trustworthy areas using Smart Lock. A secure screen lock is required to make good use of this function.

- Lock screen settings: Here you may change your screen lock settings. A secure screen lock is required for this function to work properly.

Clock and information

You may configure the Lock screen to display clock, time, and other important features by following these steps.

- o To begin, open the Settings app and then choose

  Lock screen from the list of available options:

- Enhance your wallpaper experience by activating extra features such as the Guide page and Dynamic lock screen.

- You have complete control over the look of your clock.

- While you're on the go, you may use your device's built-in clock to keep track of time.

- Widgets: Customize your home screen with beautiful widgets that make it easy to access specific functions.

- Personalize your phone so that it displays your contact information, including your email address, phone number, and other facts.

- Notifications: Choose which alerts you would want to be shown on the Lock screen.

- You may customize the Lock screen to use shortcuts from certain applications by going to the "Shortcuts" menu.

- For the Lock screen, make sure you're using the most recent version of the program.

Find My Mobile

To locate a misplaced or stolen device, enable this function. You may remotely erase all of your device's data and keep tabs on it using this capability. In order for this functionality to function, you will need a Samsung account and to have Google Location activated on your device. You may discover more information at samsung.com/us/support/owners/app/find-mymobile.

Turn on Find My Mobile

Step by step, enable the Find My Mobile function.

1. Pick Biometrics and security>Find My Mobile in the Settings app to begin.

2. After you log in to your Samsung account, you may turn it on by selecting the On symbol.

3. The following choices will be displayed to you:

- Remote Unlock: By enabling Samsung to save your PIN, Pattern, or Password, you can remotely manage your phone.

- If your phone's battery life dips below a certain threshold, you may set it to submit its last known position to the Find My Mobile service.

- Update Find My Mobile: Verify that you are using the most recent software version and look for any available upgrades.

Find My Device

Once you enable this option, your smartphone is safeguarded against loss. The gadget may be remotely hacked and its data deleted over the internet. must use this function, you'll need a Samsung account and must have Google Location switched on.

1. Find My Device may be accessed by opening your phone's Settings app, going to ⬤ Biometrics and security, and finally tapping the corresponding button.

- Follow the on-screen prompts to log in to your Google account; otherwise, this functionality will not function.

2. Here are the available options:

- The Find My Device app is available on the Google Play Store.

- Internet connectivity is required to see it on the web.

- One option is to use Google to search for it.

Secure Folder

Make a safe folder to prevent unauthorized individuals from accessing your device and discovering critical information. In order to set up a protected folder, you'll also have to sign it using your Samsung Account.

1. Press Biometrics and security in the Settings app, then select Secure Folder to begin.

2. The steps to create the folder are displayed on the screen.

Private share

When you share files using the private share, you may stop anyone with access to your device from re-sharing your material.

o To begin, launch the Settings app. Then, go to Biometrics and security. Tap Private sharing.

Then, follow the on-screen instructions to add files.

Install unknown apps

Apps that come from unknown sources might have their installation allowed.

1. Go to ⬤ Biometrics and security > Install unknown applications in the Settings app.

2. Press the "Allow from this source" button once you've chosen an app or website.

TIP: You put your smartphone and personal information at risk when you install applications from strange sources.

Encrypt and Decrypt SD card

Encrypt your SD card to keep sensitive data safe.

1. To begin encrypting the SD card, go to Settings. Then, touch on ⬤ Biometrics and security. Finally, choose the option to either encrypt or decrypt the SD card.

2. Turn on the option to encrypt the SD card.

3. To code all the data on your SD card, just follow the onscreen instructions.

TIP: A factory data reset will not compromise encrypted SD cards. Before performing a factory data reset, ensure that the attached SD card has been decrypted.

Decrypt SD card

Before you may use the SD card in another device or do a factory data reset, decrypt it.

1. Tap Biometrics and security > Encrypt or decode SD card in the Settings menu to start decrypting your SD card.

2. Select "Decrypt SD card"

3. Simply follow the on-screen prompts to unlock the data stored on your SD card.

Password for factory data reset

Resetting your phone to its factory settings requires a password.

1. Biometrics and security > Other security options may be accessed using the Setting app.

2. Choose "Setup" > "Change Password," and then enter a new password.

Set up SIM card lock

By using a SIM card lock, you may prevent unauthorized individuals from using your SIM card in the event that it goes missing or is stolen. Carrier options might differ.

1. ⭕ Biometrics and security > Other security settings is where you should begin after opening the Settings app.

2. Pick "Set up SIM card lock" and then adhere to the on-screen prompts.

*   Choose Lock SIM card to enable this function, and then press Change SIM card PIN to create a new PIN.

View Passwords

Your smartphone may have the option to display the password alongside your input.

○ Tap on ⭕ Biometrics & security > Other security options > Make passwords visible to enable the function after launching options.

Device administration

Do this to grant administrative access to your smartphone to security features and applications.

1. To start, open the Preference app. From there, go to Biometrics and security > Other security options. Finally, choose Device admin applications.

2. To go into administrator mode for the device, choose the appropriate option.

Credential storage

You have the ability to manage the trusted security certificates that are loaded on your smartphone.

o To start, go to Preferences. Then, under Biometrics and security, tap Other security settings. Here you may find the following options:

• You may categorize your storage options by clicking the "Storage type" button.

• See installed security certificates: You may enable this feature in your phone's settings when you're in the recovery mode or while you're installing additional certificates.

- View the user certificates that validate your phone under the "User certificates" section.

- The first option is to install the certificate directly from your device or phone's storage.

- Here you may reset your password and erase all of your credentials from your phone.

Permission Manager

When you initially launch an app on your smartphone, it will ask for permission to use certain features. For example, before an app can use your camera, microphone, or location, it must first have permission.

1. To access the settings, open the app and go to the privacy section. From there, choose Permission manager.

2. You may choose which permissions to be alerted about by selecting a category and then tapping on an application.

Samsung Privacy

You may provide Samsung with diagnostic information about your phone if it's experiencing technical issues.

1. Start by opening the Settings app. From there, tap on 🔒 Privacy.

2. Under Samsung, choose the "Customize" option.

- View Samsung's privacy information at Samsung Privacy.

- One option is to use Samsung's customization service, which allows users to create personalized content and suggestions.

- In the event that you are experiencing technical difficulties with your phone, you have the option to transmit diagnostic data to Samsung for diagnosis.

Date and Time

Here are the simple procedures to set the time either manually or automatically.

- To access the date and time, open the Settings app, and then click the ⬡ General management button. Consider the following options:
- Time and date automatically updated: Under typical use, your device will get changes to the time and date via your wireless network. Disabling automatic date and time will reveal the following options:
- Change the time zone: Choose a different time zone from the available options.
- Put the current date in the "Set date" field.
- In the "Set time" field, type in the exact moment in time.
- To display the time in a 24-hour format, choose that option.

Reset

It is possible to erase all data from your Samsung A16 smartphone.

Reset all settings

Follow these steps to return the gadget to its factory default settings:

NOTE: Your personnel are safe.

1. Reset all settings may be accessed from the Starting point (Settings) by clicking General management, then tapping Reset.

2. Choose "Reset settings."

3. Just follow the on-screen prompts.

Reset network Settings

You can also return the network settings to their default.

1. To reset your network settings, go to the Start menu (Settings), then hit General management, reset, and finally pick Reset.

2. Please confirm your selection of Reset network settings.

Reset accessibility settings

Make sure all of your downloaded apps and personal data are safe before resetting accessibility settings.

1. To start, open the Settings app. From the ⬒ General management menu, choose "Reset." Then, choose "Reset accessibility settings."

2. Scroll down to "Reset accessibility setting" and tap the "Confirm" button.

Auto restart at set times

You have the option to schedule a restart for your Samsung A16 smartphone.

NOTE: None of your saved data will be recoverable if your device reboots.

1. Tap "⬒ General management," then "Reset," and finally "Auto restart at set times" in the Settings app to begin.

2. Select ⬓ and choose from the following settings to enable auto restart:

• Choose the day of the week you'd want your device to restart by going to the "Days" menu.

• Choose the exact time of day that you would like your device to reset under the "Time" option.

Factory data reset

Your entire media library, including photos, movies, music, and even your Google account information, will be deleted when you do a factory data reset on your device. Data saved on an external SD card is the only data that will remain intact.

Before resetting your device:

1. Make sure anything you wish to keep has been transferred to the external storage.

2. Verify your login credentials by logging into your Google Account.

To reset your phone:

1. Select [icon] General management > Reset > Factory data reset from the Settings screen to begin the procedure.

2. To reset, click the Reset button and then follow the on-screen instructions.

3. If the phone reboots while setting it up, just follow the on-screen instructions.

Google Device Protection

When you go into your Google account and enable the lock screen, this function will be active. Verifying your identity with your Google account prevents unauthorized access to your device's factory data.

Enable Google Device Protection

"Google Device Protection" requires a Google account login and the configuration of a lock screen before it can be enabled.

Disable Google Device Protection

If you want to off Google Device Protection, you need to log out of all your Google accounts.

To remove Google Accounts:

1. Begin by opening the Settings app. From there, choose 🔄 Accounts and backup. Then, hit Manage accounts. Finally, press [Google Account].

2. Deactivate the account.

To remove a secure screen lock:

1. Start by opening the Settings app. From there, choose Lock screen > Screen lock type.
2. Please choose None or swipe.